A Note to Parents

DK READERS is a compelling program for beginning
readers, designed in conjunction with leading literacy
experts, including Dr. Linda Gambrell, Professor of Education
at Clemson University. Dr. Gambrell has served as President
of the National Reading Conference, the College Reading
Association, and the International Reading Association.

Beautiful illustrations and superb full-color photographs
combine with engaging, easy-to-read stories to offer a fresh
approach to each subject in the series. Each DK READER is
guaranteed to capture a child's interest while developing his
or her reading skills, general knowledge, and love of reading.

The five levels of DK READERS are aimed at different
reading abilities, enabling you to choose the books that are
exactly right for your child:

Pre-level 1: Learning to read
Level 1: Beginning to read
Level 2: Beginning to read alone
Level 3: Reading alone
Level 4: Proficient readers

The "normal" age at which
a child begins to read can be
anywhere from three to eight years
old. Adult participation through
the lower levels is very helpful for
providing encouragement,
discussing storylines, and sounding
out unfamiliar words.

No matter which level you select,
you can be sure that you are
helping your child learn to read,
then read to learn!

LONDON, NEW YORK, MUNICH,
MELBOURNE, AND DELHI

Editor John Searcy
Designer Jessica Park
Managing Art Editor Michelle Baxter
Publishing Director Beth Sutinis
Production Controller Charlotte Oliver
DTP Coordinator Kathy Farias

Reading Consultant
Linda Gambrell, PhD

First American Edition, 2009
09 10 11 12 13 10 9 8 7 6 5 4 3 2 1
Published in the United States by DK Publishing
375 Hudson Street, New York, New York 10014

DK books are available at special discounts when purchased in bulk
for sales promotions, premiums, fund-raising, or educational use.
For details, contact:
DK Publishing Special Markets
375 Hudson Street
New York, New York 10014
SpecialSales@dk.com

A catalog record for this book is available
from the Library of Congress.

ISBN: 978-0-7566-5552-5 (Paperback)
ISBN: 978-0-7566-5553-2 (Hardcover)

Printed and bound in the U.S.A. by Lake Book Manufacturing, Inc.

The publisher would like to thank the following for their kind
permission to reproduce their photographs:
a=above, b=below/bottom, c=center, l=left, r=right, t=top
Alamy Images: JupiterImages/Brand X 32bl. **AP Photo:** Ron
Edmonds 2t, 24–25, 26–27; J. Scott Applewhite 4; Gerald Herbert 12;
Susan Walsh 27tr; Jae Hong 29; Haraz N. Ghanbari 32tr. **Bridgeman
Art Library:** Collection of the New-York Historical Society, USA 8–9.
Corbis: Ralf-Finn Hestoft 1, 14–15; Jim Young/Reuters 2b, 28; Callie
Shell/Obama Transition Office/Handout/Reuters 5; Leslie E. Kossoff/
Pool 6–7; Michael Christopher Brown 9tr; Matthew Cavanaugh/epa
10–11; Handout/Reuters 17br; David Bergman 20; Pat Benic/epa
22tl; Thomas Mukoya/Reuters 22br; Martin H. Simon 23; Gary
Hershorn/Reuters 30–31; Pete Souza/White House/Handout 32cl;
32cr. **DK Images:** Angus Osborn/Rough Guides 3, 7br. **Getty Images:**
Charles Ommanney 2c, 18, 19; Mandel Ngan/AFP 16–17; Jim Bourg-
Pool 21; Alex Wong 24t. **Library of Congress:** 13.

All other images © Dorling Kindersley
For further information see: www.dkimages.com

Discover more at
www.dk.com

DK READERS

BEGINNING TO READ ALONE

2

Inauguration Day

Written by Laaren Brown

DK Publishing

On a cold morning in January,
an American family woke up
and got ready for their busy day.
The father had a very
important new job.
He was starting that afternoon.
His daughters called him Dad,
but by the end of the day the

*Blair House,
where the
Obama
family stayed
before they
moved to the
White House*

Sasha   *Malia*   *Michelle*   *Barack*

rest of the world would call him
President Barack Obama.
It was Inauguration Day!

That morning, Barack Obama and his wife, Michelle, went to see their new home, the White House. President George W. Bush and his wife, Laura, welcomed them. Soon, the Bushes would leave the White House and the Obamas would move in.

White House
The White House was completed in 1800. Every president except George Washington has lived there.

Every four years, the United States holds an election so voters can choose the next president. Inauguration Day is the day the new president begins his term. Long ago, when George Washington became

George Washington

Inaugurations

An inauguration is a ceremony in which a president takes office. It's a time for parades, music, and speeches.

the first president, Inauguration Day was held in the spring. Now it is always on January 20.

January 20, 2009, was a special Inauguration Day. Barack Obama was going to become the first African-American president in the

history of the United States.
For days, people had flooded
into Washington, D.C.
They wanted to wish him
good luck in his new job!

Barack Obama's daughters, Malia and Sasha, were excited, too. A few days before the inauguration, the family visited the Lincoln Memorial. They looked at the big statue of Abraham Lincoln. Malia said to her father, "First African-American president. Better make it good."

Abraham Lincoln
Abraham Lincoln freed the slaves during the Civil War. He is admired as one of the greatest presidents in American history.

Presidents are sworn in at a
building called the Capitol.
It sits at the end of a long park
called the National Mall.
For months, people had worked
hard to prepare the Mall
and the Capitol for the big day.
Lots of guests were coming!

Now, everything was ready.
Barack and Michelle left the
White House with George and
Laura to go to the Capitol.
Workers in the White House
packed up the Bush family's things.
Then they unpacked everything
the new first family would need,
from Barack Obama's suits to
Sasha Obama's socks.

Presidential limos
Presidents usually ride
around Washington
in special limousines.
The huge 2009 model
was called the Beast.

Inside the Capitol, Malia and
Sasha waited with their parents.
Outside, on the Mall and
beyond, nearly two million
people waited, too.

All across the country, all around
the world, millions of Americans

were waiting for
Barack Obama
to become
the 44th
President of
the United
States.

On the frosty Mall, people stood shoulder to shoulder. Giant TV screens showed important guests taking their seats. Three former presidents were there, along with their vice presidents. Soon, Malia and Sasha appeared, smiling and happy. Then Michelle Obama arrived.

Former president Bill Clinton and his wife, Hillary

And finally . . . Barack Obama
stepped out from the Capitol.
The crowd went wild!
Everyone cheered and clapped.

Aretha Franklin

A preacher spoke. "We are so grateful to live in this land . . . where the son of an African immigrant can rise to the highest level," he said. Some people wept with joy. The great Aretha Franklin sang,

Proud family
Barack Obama's father was from Kenya in Africa. All over Kenya, people celebrated Obama's inauguration.

"My country, 'tis of thee . . ."
Then it was time to swear in
the new vice president.
Joe Biden stepped up and took
his oath of office.

Joe Biden

At last, Barack Obama was ready to be sworn in as president. He put his left hand on a Bible.

Lincoln Bible

Abraham Lincoln used this Bible at his inauguration in 1861. Barack Obama chose to use the same one in 2009.

Michelle Obama held it.
Malia and Sasha stood next to
their mother.
Their father raised his right
hand as he spoke:
"I, Barack Hussein Obama . . ."

The oath took less than a minute.
At the end, everyone cheered.
America had a new president!

Next, President Obama gave a speech. He asked Americans

to be hopeful and to help him make the country better. When he was done, Sasha gave her father a big thumbs-up. "That was a pretty good speech, Dad!" she said.

That afternoon, there was a
parade in Washington.
Barack and Michelle Obama
walked in the street, waving.
Then they watched from a
platform with Malia and Sasha.
Many marching bands played.
One was from Barack Obama's
old high school in Hawaii.

That night, there were many parties.
The president and the first lady danced.
Later, there would be many people to help and many problems to solve.
But at this moment, everyone felt proud and happy to be an American, with a new president and a new family in the White House.

Inauguration facts

Months before Inauguration Day, people gather for the First Nail Ceremony. They hammer the very first nail into the platform that will hold the new president.

During Barack Obama's oath of office, the word *faithfully* was spoken out of place. On January 21, Obama took the oath again. This time it was perfect!

Abraham Lincoln was the first president to invite an African-American to his inauguration. His guest was the abolitionist Frederick Douglass.

Legend says that on the night of the inauguration, the statues of great Americans in the Capitol come to life and dance.